1 in the basket

Many years after the death of Joseph, the Israelites were still living in the far-off land of Egypt. It was not their home and sometimes they wondered if they would ever go back to the land which God had given them.

The new king of Egypt treated the Israelites as slaves. They had to work all day under the hot sun in the fields or building great cities.

But the king of Egypt was worried. Each year there were more and more Israelites being born. One day there might be so many Israelites that they would overrun his land.

So he ordered his people to throw any new-born Israelite baby boys into the great River Nile.

The Israelites were terrified and did all they could to protect their children.

One brave mother hid her baby son until he was three months old. Then she made a small waterproof basket, just big enough to hide him in, and placed the little child in the basket by the reeds at the side of the river.

The little baby's big sister, Miriam, stayed nearby on the river bank and bravely watched the precious basket. She knew that if anyone caught her or found the baby, she would be in deep trouble.

Then she saw the princess of Egypt and her friends walking along by the river. The princess was preparing to take a bath. Miriam was frightened, but she kept on watching.

The Baby in the Basket

Open up this re-usable picture. Decorate it with the stickers in this book!

Now use your stickers!

Have fun with your Collect-a-Bible-Story!

1. Read the whole story.
2. Carefully remove the re-usable stickers.
3. Complete the picture. Display it in your room!

Collect the whole series!

Every Collect-a-Bible-Story comes with re-usable stickers and a picture for you to decorate. Make sure you get each one!

The princess soon caught sight of the mysterious basket. Moments later she was cuddling the little child. "It's a little Israelite baby!" cried the princess.

At that moment Miriam did something very brave. She came out of her hiding place and said, "Would you like someone to help you look after that baby?"

The princess was delighted by the idea! So Miriam raced back and fetched her own mother. The pair of them were back with the princess in moments and soon the little baby was being nursed by his own, real, mother.

Of course, the Egyptian princess had no idea that this was the baby's mother and she agreed to pay her for looking after the child.

The princess also arranged that as soon as the baby was old enough, she would adopt him, and take him to live with her at the palace.

Before long, the young boy went to live with the princess and was brought up as an Egyptian child. Because the princess had rescued him from the river, she decided to call him "Moses" which means "pulled out".

Although he was being brought up by an Egyptian princess and living in luxury, Moses never forgot he was an Israelite.

God planned to use him to rescue his people and lead them out of Egypt, into the special land he had promised them.